HOW RECESSION IMPACTS SOCIAL CRIME BEHAVIOR

JOHN LOK

Copyright © John Lok
All Rights Reserved.

This book has been published with all efforts taken to make the material error-free after the consent of the author. However, the author and the publisher do not assume and hereby disclaim any liability to any party for any loss, damage, or disruption caused by errors or omissions, whether such errors or omissions result from negligence, accident, or any other cause.

While every effort has been made to avoid any mistake or omission, this publication is being sold on the condition and understanding that neither the author nor the publishers or printers would be liable in any manner to any person by reason of any mistake or omission in this publication or for any action taken or omitted to be taken or advice rendered or accepted on the basis of this work. For any defect in printing or binding the publishers will be liable only to replace the defective copy by another copy of this work then available.

2019 July Print Published
All rights reserved. This book or any portion thereof may not be reproduced or used in any manner whatsoever without the express written permission of the publisher except for the use of brief quotations in a book review or scholarly journal

Contents

Preface

Introduction

This book researches whether global macro economic environment change positive or negative factor will impact any countries' crime rate to be raised or reduced. Has it relationship between global macro economic environment and young unemployed people whose behaviors change, e.g. attempting stealing when they encounter long term unemployment suitation or attempting to sell illegal drug to earn income or performing anit-social damage behavior to influence convenient road transportation and working people need catch amy public transportation tools etc. traffic jam manual causing anti-social damage behavior? Is poor macro economic environment main factor to influence crime number increases ?

Readers can make more accurate analysis to judge whether macro economic environment variable factor will influence social crime behaviors occurs easily after you read this book.

Prologue

Table Of Content

I

Unemployment causes crime

Why does global macro economic environment become worse, it will bring many countries' unemployment rates raise as well as it can cause crime rate number rises in possible? I believe that they have case and effect relationship. In most countries, unemployment is higher today than it was in the 1960s. Why are these such large variations in unemployment, it brings more crime after 1960s? I shall indicate the reasons as below:

(1) Hiring costs raise unemployment as firms become more anxious to keep the workers they have,which puts upward pressure on wages. So, when the global societies employers feel any costs are increasing after 1960s, e.g. manufacturing cost, rent cost, office and/or office electricity cost , goods transportation cost , even wage cots etc. hen, many employers will choose to dismiss many workers and unemployment rate will be raised. When many workers lose jobs for long time. Social crime number will increase,

in special, the low educational and low skillful workers. Their crime mind and crime behaviors will be caused by long term unemployment.

(2) Generous unemployment benefits may make workers more selective in their job search and raise unemployment. IN fact, after 1960s, global macro economic environment had been improving from manufacturing industry to service, than high technological industries development both. It will cause the developing countries, such as Africa, China, Hong Kong, Korea etc., their low education and low skillful workers lose jobs suddenly, due to their manufacturing skills won't be popular needed to employers. For example, old cloth drwssing machines will be replaced from new high technological cloth dressing machines, old car manufacturing factory method will be replaced by high technological artificial intelligent car manufacturing method. When the low manufacturing skillful workers can not find any manufacturing jobs to match their manufactury skills in their job search process. Then, in long term unemployment situation, the high technolobical development factor will cause the low manufacturing skillful workers have crime or anti-social psychological mind to cause crime behaviors easily.

(3) Mismatch between worker skills and labor demand means that unemployed workers have differenties competing for jobs which will raise the level of unemployment. Similiar , due to global macro economic environment changes, e.g. many high technological skillful workers number increases, but the supply of high technological skillful workers number can not grow rapidly. So, it brings the shortage of high technological skillful labor supply. Otherwise, in global societies , many low technological skillful workers, they do not continue to

learn any kinds of high technological knowledge to prepare to find any high technological jobs easily. So, global societies bring the mismatch between worker skills and labor demand. Consequently, it many bring many low technological skillful workers still lose jobs for long time , Then, their crime behaviors will also be influenced to raise in possible.

(4) Lacking a well-functioning education system and active labor market policy could potentialy raise mismatch and unemployed. The reason is easy to understand. For Hong Kong example, HK crime rate is increasing after 1960s. although, HK's manufacturing industry is replaced by monetary, service industries maninly nowadays. HK lacks a well functioning education system to educate the low educational level and low skillful youngers to be trained their skills to prepare to do further high technological development industry. So, HK's social weakness is a lack of high technological jobs well-functioning education system. It can train many youngers to do high technological jobs in active labor market.

Nowadays, HK has many employers need high technolgical workers in active labor market. It will cause many HK high technological businesses can not find any high technological workers easily in HK. Then, they will choose to find overseas high technological workers to replace HK domestic workers, as well as it will cause HK high technological workers' wages to be reduced. Otherwise, overseas high technological workers' wages will be raised . Even longer time , HK many high technological workers will lose jobs, because their skills can be replaced from overseas high technological workers easily. If their demand still need HK employers raise their salaries to compare to overseas high technological workers' salaries . Due to this global macro high technological workers demand increasing factor influences to HK, so China, or other developing high technological job markets. Then, it may cause many developing countries' high technological workers lose thier jobs, due to the developed countries' high technological workers can be replaced to do their job more easy, even their salaries demand is lower to compare to the developing countries high technological workers' salaries demand. So, when the developing countries ' high technological workers feel unfair, they lose jobs, due to overseas developed countries' high technological wotkers are replaced. It will cause that they will choose to do crime behavior in society more easier.

Also, HK's job security legislation is poor to comapre Western countries. For example, US, UK, New Zealand, Australia etc. Western countries. They have good citizen security legislation. All those Western countries' citizen own unemployment assistance, when they lose jobs to do in long time or they unemploy long time. Then, they have authority to need their governments to give unemployment assistance. If they have no any unemployment or they have less unemployment before 60 or 65 retirement age. Then, after 60 or 65 age, their government will still give them money for life assistance per week, till to they die. Otherwise, HK government only have job security legislation to reduce employee individual 5% of salary for MPF (mututary provident fund) and employee's 5 % salary for MPF maximum per month for their retirement benefit. HK government won't give HK citizen money for life assistance after 65 retirement age. If the HK citizen earned less salary before 65 age, then it is not enough to provide social welfare assistance to any HK citizen after they reach 65 age in possible. So, it explains that why some HK old

people will do crime behaviors more easily.
Does long-term unemployment cause social problem? There is no question that high unemployment is a major social problem, but zero unemployment is neither feasible nor a desirable object for poicy. In fact, it is natural and acceptable that some workers are unemployed between different jobs. For example, when one waiter is dismisses or unemployed , due to his restaurant employer loses business or another waiter is employed different reasons . Then, he spends more six months to seek the same waiter job, but he still can not find any same job easily. Then, he chooses to learn any similar waiter service skills, e.g. hotel waiter service skill. He needs to spend another six months to lean the new hotel waiter service and attitude knowledge, because restaurant waiter service skil is very diffeent to hotel waiter service skill need. He needs to learn how to serve hotel restaurant clients. Thus, in this year unemployment minimum period, it includes the six months seeling restaurant waiter job period and another six months learning hotel waiter job learing period, this restaurant waiter unemployed worker won;t earn any salary in this year. It means that long-term unemployment period to this career seeker. Also, it is rational for this restaurant waiter unemployed worker not to take the first restaurant waiter job, he can get , but to attempt to learn hotel restaurant waiter service knowledge to wait for a hotel restaurant waiter job employment in possible, where he can use his specific competence and be rewarded for this with a reasonable waiter occupation wage.
If this restaurant unemployed waiter was occasionally unemployed for a few weeks between jobs, this is not necessarily a big social problem. The really serious socal problem occurs when workers are stuck in unemployment

for many months or even years, such as this restaurant unemployed waiter case, he has one year unemployment period at least. It includes, the six months without salary restaurant waiter job search period and another six months without hotel restuarant waiter learning period. Moreover, he also need to pay tuition for this hotel restaurant waiter course as well as he also needs to pass the practice and paper test of hotel restaurant waiter course in order to earn this certificate of their hotel restaurant waiter occupation and he can find any hotel restaurant waiter job more easy. However, if he can not pass this course, then he needs to do choice either paying tuition to study this course again or he can attempt to find the same past restaurant waiter job again or he can attempt to learn another new skill to further change his new occupation career. Then , it brings this question : Does long term unemployment cause or influence this restaurant waiter perform crime behavior in society ? I believe that the answer is depended that how long in typical worker will be unemployed. To see what determines the expected duration of unemployment , assume for simplicity that workers who find a job in a particular month start working at the end of that month, so that all workers who become unemployed remain unemployed for least one month. So, the duration of unemployment depends on three factors as well as these three factors can influence any unemployed workers choose to do crime behaviors in society more easily. They include as below:

(1) Whether the country is a higher rate or lower rate of unemployment in society means , that there are more workers competing for available jobs in the country and less chance to find a jon, which needs a longer duration of unemployment. For Hong Kong employment market

example, nowadays, there are many young people (university students) choose to study monetary subject to do bank jobs, or seek further monetary , share investment monetary related occupations to work. Hence, there are more monetary related subject, e.g. finance, accounting university graduate students compete for any available monetary related jobs in HK, but in fact, HK monetary related investment jobs number is not enough or supply shortage.

It depends on macro economic environment whether there are many overseas investors choose to set up their businesses in HK or there are less overseas investors choose to set up their businesses in HK. So, if the year, there was less overseas investors number in HK. Then , it may cause any kinds of monetary related jobs number as less to supply in HK job market. If the year, there were a many monetary subject graduate students increased. It causes the effect of a longer duration of unemployment to the year monetary subject university graduate students in HK. Then, the any related monetary crime cases may also increase , due to these HK monetary subject university students can not find any monetary related jobs in HK easily. They do not want to find other jobs to replace monetary jobs, it may be due to low salary is paid, unsatisfactory workin environment, without monetary job duties practice chance satisfies their further career development need. If HK macro economic environment was continue poor after the year. It kept to two year, threee years, even more than five years poor macro economic period. Then, the overseas investors number to HK will decrease, even many HK overseas investors also planned to forgive their businesses to be close in HK. It means that they choose to close their HK businesses and their offices were left. Then, it will influence any HK monetary related jobs number will reduce, but as the same time every year, HK monetary major subject unviersity students number is also increasing. Consequently, it will cause or influence any kinds of monetary crime cases will be increased to HK by the long term unemployment to many HK university major monetary subject graduate students factor.

(2) A high rate of separations (people leaving jobs) means that there are more job opening, so the duration of unemployment decreases. It means that when the country has there working people often change old jobs or they planned to find new jobs to replace current jobs or they expect to change another new jobs reasons. It implies that the country's economy is improving or better to compare before. There are more job openings, many employers create different kinds of new jobs to satisfy their businesses needs. So the duration of unemployment will be influenced to decrease in possible. Because many new creative jobs number is caused. Working people have much chance to attempt to find another new jobs to replace their current jobs in the country.

Even, some working people are doing one job, which can give reasonable wage and it can have more promotion chance in this current job. They will still choose to find another new jobs , it may be that they feel there are many new creative jobs , which can bring new exciting feeling, which can bring nre exciting feeing , more satisfactory feeling , more fun feeling , more successful feeling, more interesting feeling to compare their current jobs . So, it is not only higher salary factor to influence them to change current jobs.

For US job market example, US macro economic environment has been improving very good, many new creative jobs are increasing, e.g. in (AI) job aspect, artificial intelligence scientist , (AI) engineer, big data gathering scientist, non-manual automatic (AI) controlling worker, e.g. artificial intelligence factory machine controlling workers, in medicine job aspect, e.g. drug researcher, DNA cell science researcher, brain doctor, occupational psychological doctor, space science researcher or space scientist etc. creative occupations. There new creative occupations can supply enough jobs to many US high educational level graduate students and they can encourage them to change their current more easily.

In fact, US , these are many different occupations, scientists have jobs, they are doing, but they still expect or plan to change another new similar or different new creative jobs easily. Because the US high education new creative science jobs supply number is more than the US any science graduate students number in US labor market nowadays. So, it explains that why US crime number is decreasing nowadays. Because US has good macro economic environment. US itself country's any new creative job supply number and non creative job supply number must have more than the US graduate student number every year. So, US has good macro economic environment to supply enough jobs number to any US low educational and high educating level young people to job.

Consequently, it causes crime number reduced in US society nowadays. Otherwisem HK has less creative jobs to be supplied to let HK young university graduate students, as well as HK university graduate students number is increasing, but university level jobs number is decreasing at this moment. So, it explains that only HK society increases crime number easily nowadays.

All of above analysis, I assume that the standard measure

of long term unemployment id the number of workers who have been unemployed for more than 12 months as well as they feel worry to earn enough income to support their basic essential needs, such as eating need, living need, but it excludes non essential needs, such as entertainment need, travelling need, education need.

So, when these countries young people feel long time unemployment to cause they can not have enough income to support their basic essential needs, then It may influence they choose to do crime behaviors in themselves societies more easily. I shall indicate how any why high turnover and low turnover countries will bring high or low crome behavioral causes in some countries themselves societies.

OECD(2011) concluded the high turnover countries, abourt 10 % of unemployment is long term . So it brings low crime rate . Otherwise, in the low turnover countries, 30 to 60% of the unemployed have beed out of jobs for more than one year, it will bring high crime rate. It explains that it has direct relationship between crime rate number and unemployment rate more than one year number from the average 1999 to 2008 more or less than one year unemployment rate statistics. It indicates that the average 1999 to 2008 period, these low turnover countries have high unemployment rate more than a year , then these low turnover countries crime rate will be influenced to increase also, these low turnvoer or high unemployment countries include: Turkey, France, Netherlands, Greece, Cyech Republic, Hungery, Slovall Republic, Germany, Italy, Portugal, Belgium, Poland, Spain, Switerland, Ireland, Finland, Austia, Japan, United Kingdom. So , these countries‘ crime rare has been increasing in this period. Otherwise, these high turnover countries or low unemployment rare more than one year, then these high turnover countries crime rate will be influenced to decrease also. There high turnover or low unemployment countries include: Iceland, Norway, United States, Mexico, New Zealand, Canada, Denmark, Australia, Sweden.

In conclusion, it explains that when the country's macro economy environment is improved of better, then it has more high education or low education level jobs to be supplied to let many young people have any kinds of jobs to work easily. Them, it will bring low unemployment effect and low crime rate effect both . Consequently, unemployment has relationship to cause crime rate rises or reduced in possible in any countries' societies.

Reference

OECD , employment and labor market statistics, OECD , 27 April 2011. source http://www.oecdilibrary.org/statistics.

II

Relationship between a recession and crime

Has it relationship between a recession and crime? To answer this relationship question, I shall explain what is macroeconomics. Then, you will give more clear understanding why and why recession will impact social crime behaviors to bre rasied in possible.

What is Macroeconomics? Macroeconomics is a branch of economics that studies how the aggregate economy behaves. In macroeconomics, economy-wide
phenomena are examined such as inflation, price levels, rate of economic growth, national income, gross domestic product
(GDP), and changes in unemployment.On the other hand,

microeconomics looks at the behavior of individual actors in an economy (like people, households, industries, etc). Macroeconomics is the branch of economics that deals with the structure, performance, behavior,and decision-making of the whole, or aggregate, economy, instead of focusing on individual markets.The two main areas of macroeconomic study are long term economic growth and shorter term business cycles.

There are two sides to the study of economics: macroeconomics and microeconomics. As the term implies, macroeconomics looks at the overall, big picture scenario of the economy. Put simply, it focuses on the way the economy performs as a whole, and then analyzes how different sectors of the economy relate to one another to understand how the economy functions. This includes looking at variables like unemployment, GDP, and inflation.

Macroeconomists develop models explaining relationships between these factors. Such macroeconomic models, and the forecasts they produce, are used by government entities to aid in the construction and evaluation of economic policy, by businesses to set strategy in domestic and global markets, and by investors to predict and plan for movements in various asset markets.

Given the enormous scale of government budgets and the impact of economic policy on consumers and businesses, macroeconomics clearly concerns itself with significant issues. Properly applied, economic theories can offer illuminating insights on how economies function and the long-term consequences of particular policies and decisions. Macroeconomic theory can also help individual businesses and investors make better decisions through a

more thorough understanding of what motivates other parties and how to best maximize utility and scarce resources.It is also important to understand the limitations of economic theory. Theories are often created in a vacuum and lack
certain real-world details like taxation, regulation and transaction costs. The real world is also decidedly complicated and their matters of social preference and conscience that do not lend themselves to mathematical analysis.

Even with the limits of economic theory, it is important and worthwhile to follow the major macroeconomic indicators like GDP,
inflation and unemployment. The performance of companies, and by extension their stocks, is significantly influenced by the economic
conditions in which the companies operate and the study of macroeconomic statistics can help an investor make better decisions and spot turning points.

- Specific Areas of Crime rate increasing ,due to poor macro economy environment influences

Macroeconomics is a rather broad field, but two specific areas of research are representative of this discipline. The first area
is the factors that determine long-term economic growth, or increases in the national income. The other involves the causes and
consequences of short-term fluctuations in national income and employment, also known as the business cycle,

such as researching whether recession will cause crime rate rising issue.

Economic growth refers to an increase in aggregate production in an economy. Macroeconomists study economic growth with an eye toward understanding the factors that either promote or retard economic growth in order to support economic policies that will
support growth, development, and rising living standards. Growth is commonly modeled as a function of physical capital, human capital, labor force, and technology. So, when economic growth is raising, then unemployment rate will decrease in possible.

- Business Positive or negative Cycles and

the country's macro economic environment is good and bad relationship

A long term macroeconomic growth trends, the levels and rates-of-change of major macroeconomic variables such as employment and national output go through occasional fluctuations up or down, expansions and recessions, in a phenomenon known as the business cycle.

- Macroeconomics vs. Microeconomics , what can influence crime rate more?

Macroeconomics differs from microeconomics, which focuses on smaller factors that affect choices made by individuals and companies.Factors studied in both microeconomics and macroeconomics typically have an influence on one another. For example, the unemployment level in the economy as a whole has an effect on the supply of workers from which a company can hire.

A key distinction between micro and macroeconomics is that macroeconomic aggregates can sometimes behave in ways that are very different or even the opposite of the way that analogous microeconomic variables do.Meanwhile, microeconomics looks at economic tendencies, or what can happen when individuals make certain choices. Individuals are typically classified into subgroups, such as buyers, sellers, and business owners. These actors interact with each other according to the laws of supply and demand for resources, using money and interest rates as pricing mechanisms for coordination

- What factors Cause of recessions ?

A recession implies a fall in real GDP. An official definition of a recession is
a period of negative economic growth for two consecutive quarters. Recessions are
primarily caused by a fall in aggregate demand (AD).
This demand-side shock could be due to several factors, such as

· A financial crisis. If banks have a shortage of liquidity, they reduce lending – this reduces investment

· A rise in interest rates – increases the cost of borrowing and reduces demand

· Fall in asset prices. – negative wealth effect leads to less spending

· Fall in consumer/business confidence also exacerbated by negative multiplier effect.

· Appreciation in exchange rate – exports less competitive

· Fiscal austerity – when government cuts spending

Recessions can also be caused by

· Supply-side shock, e.g. rise in oil prices cause inflation and lower spending power.

For example, in US, bank failures led to a fall in the money supply and deflationary pressures.Bank failures also caused lost confidence and discourage investment.

· Negative multiplier effect – initial fall in spending caused a knock on effect throughout the economy.

There were no automatic stabilisers. People were made unemployed and so started spending less themselves. For example , causes of UK recessions1981 recession was caused by:

1.High value of the pound which made exports more expensive and reduced demand for exports.This recession particularly impacted on British manufacturing. The Pound soared due to the discovery of North Sea Oil but also the high interest rates.

2.High-interest rates. In 1979, inflation in the UK was over 15%. The new Conservative government was committed to reducing high inflation they inherited. They pursued a tight monetary policy (higher interest rates)
and tight fiscal policy (higher taxes, lower government spending. This reduced inflation but at the cost of falling spending, investment and output.interest-rates.

3.Tight Fiscal Policy. To control inflation the government were committed to reducing the levels of Government borrowing.

This was influenced by Monetarist beliefs that controlling excess government borrowing was essential to the economy. Therefore the
government increased taxes which reduced the disposable income of consumers and therefore reduced consumer spending.

A recession occurs when there is a fall in economic growth for two consecutive quarters. However, if growth is very low there will be increased spare capacity and increased unemployment; people will feel there is a recession. A key feature in determining the rate of economic growth is the level of consumer and business confidence. If confidence was high then higher interest rates may not reduce demand. However if confidence is low and people fear they may be made unemployed, then they will start spending less, causing AD to fall (or increase at a slower rate). Therefore this shows that expectations are very important and it is possible for "people to talk themselves into a recession".

For an important feature of the UK economy is international trade case. Therefore the UK would be affected by a global recession. For example, a recession in the EU would cause a fall in demand for UK exports reducing our AD (EU accounts for 60% of our trade, therefore, is important). Also, a recession in other countries would affect economic confidence if people
see the US in a recession they are worried and will spend less. However, a global recession may not cause a recession in the UK if domestic demand remains high.

Classical economists believe that any fall in Real GDP will be temporary and will end when labour markets adjust to the new price level. Classical economists argue that if there is a fall in AD then, in the short term, there will be a fall in real GDP However in the great depression of 1930s Keynes was very critical of this classical view he said that the long period of
negative growth showed that markets do not automatically clear he argued that this was for various reasons.

1.Wages are sticky downwards. Firms should cut wages to reflect lower prices but in reality, workers are very resistant to cuts in nominal wages.

2.If wages were cut in response to unemployment, workers would have less spending power, therefore AD would continue
to fall.

● Can economic crises bring rise in crime ?

Crime may peak during economic crises,
During periods of economic stress, the incidence of robbery may double, and homicide and motor vehicle theft also increase.While a consistent relationship between specific crimes and specific economic factors could not be established, the evidence shows that crime is linked to the economic climate. Such findings are consistent with criminal motivation theory, which suggests that economic stress causes an increase in criminal behaviour. The available data do not, however, support the theory of criminal opportunity, which suggests that decreased levels of production and consumption may reduce some types of crime, such as property crime, by creating fewer potential crime targets."The presence of youth gangs, the availability of weapons and potential targets, drug and alcohol consumption and the effectiveness of law enforcement all play a significant role in enabling or restraining overall crime levels",

● Relationship between a recession and crime

Criminologists say bad economies create more crime; economists say the opposite. But recent data reveals neither explanation is right.
I've been wondering if hard economic times would cause people to commit more crimes.

For example, areas with chronic poverty and unemployment tend to have high rates of child neglect and abuse. Child neglect and abuse greatly increase the risk of juveniles getting involved in crime.So areas with high rates of unemployment cop a double whammy. Their crime rates are higher because of the direct effect of unemployment and its long-term indirect effects as well.

Will the current recession produce an increase in crime? If the recession doesn't last long, there may be no effect at all.

But if the recession is deep and the pool of young long-term unemployed rises, there is every reason to expect an increase in crime.

Moreover, if this happens, the effects may last a long while. The longer you are out of work, the harder it is to find a job, and the more attractive crime becomes as an alternative source of income. And what happens this recession depends on still more factors, the most important being the income that can be earned from crime e.g.selling illegal drugs. Many thoughtful observers think that we put too many offenders in prison for too long. For some criminals, such as low-level drug dealers and former inmates returned to prison for parole violations, that may be so. The difference results not from willingness to send convicted offenders to prison in many countries' legal system

- May Economic crises trigger rise in crime ?

For the same offense, you will spend more time in prison here than in England. Canada has seen roughly the same decline in crime,

but its imprisonment rate has been relatively flat for at least two decades. Another possible reason for reduced crime is that potential

victims may have become better at protecting themselves

by equipping their homes with burglar alarms, installing extra locks on their cars, and moving into safer buildings or even safer neighborhoods.

We have only the faintest idea, however, about how common these trends are or what effects on crime they may have. Are their crime behaviors caused by economic crises ? How to explain complex link between recession and crime? For In the Environmental Protection Agency example, required oil companies to stop putting lead in gasoline. At the same time, lead in paint was banned for any new home though old buildings still have lead paint, which children can absorb.

● Why do recessions at labour market entry matter for crime? So, why is it that youth who graduate during recessions are more likely to engage in crime?

Those who leave school during a recession, when youth unemployment rates are particularly high, struggle to find a job but do not yet have financial insurance. Knock-on effects can then lead to criminal careers for the young. On the other hand, those who have criminal records early on in their career may reduce their job opportunities and expected returns in the legal labour market see. However , I agree that crime is not only a feature of the teenage years — crime rates decrease with age but do not disappear subsequently. That suggests that there is an initial effect but criminal activity is somewhat persistent over the life cycle.

● Can that persistence be explained by thc long term impact of recessions?

A typical recession leads to a 5 percentage points higher than normal unemployment rate.What is the long-term impact of graduating into such conditions? Our empirical analysis of the link between crime and unemployment at labour market entry is based on a variety of US and UK cohort and individual level data sources. We exploit cohort level data for both countries to estimate the average effect of initial labour market conditions on criminal activity of cohorts that enter the labour market at different points in time, taking into account differences in cohort composition.

- Is crime Rates increasing during recessions?

A recession is a significant decline in economic activity spread across the economy, lasting more than a few months, normally visible in production, employment, real income, and other indicators. A recession begins when the economy reaches a peak of. Have they the relationship between economic indicators and crime rates in terms of whether there is a correlation between a given indicator and crime? A positive correlation exists when increases in one variable are accompanied by increases in another variable. A negative correlation, on the other hand, occurs when increases in one variable are accompanied by decreases in another variable.

One important concept is the idea that correlation does not imply causation; the presence of two sets of data (two variables) showing similar trends does not indicate that changes in one variable cause any visible changes in the other. Instead, a correlation shows that changes in one variable can, to some extent, predict changes in another variable. For instance, while some neighborhoods may exhibit a relationship between certain types of crime and the economy, other neighborhoods may exhibit a relationship between different types of crime and the economy or may not exhibit a relationship at all.

Consequently, researchers tend to use individual economic indicators, such as the unemployment rate, as a proxy for the state of the economy. However, any given indicator may not be generalizable to the state of the economy as a whole during any one given recession or across recessions.Despite the limitations in using specific economic variables as proxies for a complex economic state, this methodology does allow researchers to isolate variables and analyze their individual.Generalizability is typically defined as the extent to which the results generated by a variable being studied can be applied to other settings, times, or groups of subjects and be expected to deliver a similar outcome. Specifically, during the most recent economic downturn, many referred to the
unemployment rate and the proportion of home foreclosures as proxies for economic health.

- What are the real factors cause the changes in the crime rates?

Impact of Unemployment on Crime
the unemployment rate is one of the most widely referenced economic indicators. In discussions of potential impacts of the economy on crime rates, many scholars and policy makers use the unemployment rate as a proxy for economic strength. Congress has shown interest in the relationship between the economy—unemployment, in particular—and crime rates since the 1970s. The most recent recession, which was accompanied by a rise in the unemployment rate, once again focused attention on the relationship between unemployment and crime rates.

Researchers and scholars have several theories concerning the relationship between
unemployment and crime. One of these theories, the

economic theory of crime, assumes that people make rational choices between legitimate activities and criminal activities as a source of economic gain. More specifically, the comparison is between the economic benefit of legitimate work versus that of violent or property crime, after accounting for crime-related costs such as incarceration. Although the theory was originally formulated with an application to all crimes, many researchers have used it in discussions of unemployment and property crime. This theory predicts a positive correlation between unemployment and property crime; in other words, that increases in the unemployment rate will be correlated with increases in property crime rates. The reason for this positive correlation, according to the economic model, is that during periods when there are fewer opportunities for legitimate income, people may turn to illegal activities, while when more jobs are available, the risks of committing a crime may be weighed against the opportunity for legitimate work.

Were a direct link between unemployment and the property crime rate, varying one would necessarily vary the other? The lack of conclusive evidence for a strong, or even significant,correlation between the two suggests that the unemployment rate may have an indirect relationship with the property crime rate. Although unemployment is correlated with overall economic conditions, it may not fully capture other key economic indicators such as work hours, employment stability, and wages. Some researchers, for example, have found that employment stability and wages may correlate more strongly with the property crime rate than does unemployment.

III

Economic Theories of Crime

What is economic theories of crime ?This brief literature review highlights three key economic frameworks that can be used to explain a persistent social problem
in modern society, crime and delinquency: the rational model, the present-oriented or myopic model, and the radical political
economic model. Based on a cost-benefit analysis, an individuals decision to engage in crime in the rational model is consistent
in the short-and long-term. Present-oriented individuals, however, focus on the short-term benefits without particular concern
for the long-term consequences of their actions. The radical political economic model focuses on the following key political and socio-economic factors that sustain crime: relative deprivation, poverty and inequality, unemployment, and class conflict.The conclusion includes

a conceptual map integrating the three frameworks.

Some economists and crime psychologists believe that crime is not limited to certain areas or to certain socioeconomic classes of society. Criminal activities take many forms, including theft, homicide,assault, fraud, embezzlement, and blackmail. So why does crime persist? Are there underlying factors that can explain criminal behavior? Can we lower the incentives for criminal behavior? Do criminals take opportunity costs of committing a crime into account? The social science field has long been interested in these questions.

This literature review focuses on the discipline of economics and its assumptions about individual decisions to commit crime. The standard assumption is that individuals who commit crimes are rational decision makers who expect to gain something from criminal activity, and this gain is greater than the expected costs associated with being caught. Most of the research in this area focuses on the effects of incentives to engage in criminal behavior and on the use of cost-benefit analysis to assess alternative policies to reduce crime. However, not all crime can be categorized as rational behavior. Socioeconomic factors are also assumed to affect crime, and alternative theories to explain criminal activities are used to challenge the standard assumption of rational behavior.

The main objective of this review is to identify the key economic frameworks that are used to explain crime and delinquency. The three key frameworks include the rational model of crime, the present-oriented or myopic model of crime, and the radical political economic model of crime.

Economists have begun to question whether the standard assumption of rational behavior holds when consideringwhy individuals engage in criminal activity. Can we really assume that all criminals make rational decisions to commit a crime? Individual preferences, psychic factors, and other motivations for crime may play an equally large role in explaining crime. However these factors are much harder to incorporate into economic models of crime. Hence, there is limited empirical research in this area. It will be interesting to see how the growing field of behavioral economics can help to explain crime and delinquency.

The three main economic models of crime are the rational model, the present oriented or myopic model, and the radical political economic model. Each model emphasizes different factors that influence individual decisions to commit crime and different ways of combating crime. What is the Rational Model of Crime mean?

Economics can be defined as a discipline that studies how scarce resources are allocated by the forces of supply and demand to meet different needs in society. In the same way, economists argue that crime is a result of individuals' making choices between using their scarce resources of time and effort in legitimate or in illegitimate activities. A key assumption is that when making these choices, individuals are rational and choose the best option based on the available information and resources. Individuals are perceived to be promoting their self-interest by rationally selecting options that provide them with the greatest benefits that are expected to exceed the costs associated with these options.

The profit from crime is traditionally measured in terms of monetary benefits but can also include physical, psychic, and other benefits. The "punishment" or costs of crime include the risk of detection, apprehension, and conviction and the severity of punishment. Economists do not refute that environmental, psychological, and biological factors may affect criminal activity. Nevertheless, they argue that individuals are free to choose between different courses of options available to them. Therefore, as long as there is a rational element of choice available, individuals who decide to commit a crime will react to changes in the probability of apprehension and the severity of punishment .This framework leads to a key concept, namely, the "opportunity cost" of crime. Any decision that involves a choice between two or more options has an opportunity cost. An opportunity cost can be defined as the value of the next best alternative within the context of making a decision. Put differently, an opportunity cost can be viewed as the benefits an individual could have received by taking an alternative decision or action. In essence, the true cost of crime for a potential criminal is the opportunity cost of spending time in prison. The opportunity cost varies among individuals irrespective of the length of incarceration.

The rational framework distinguishes between static and dynamic models of crime. In a static model, individuals compare the costs and benefits of engaging in crime in a single time period. In a dynamic model, the individual considers multiple time periods. Decisions made in the past, for example, impact the decision-making process in the present.

- Is Unemployment caused crime by poor macro economy environment factor?

Different models examine the different relationships between unemployment and crime. Some economic models assume that unemployment either lowers the opportunity costs of crime or that it increases
the need to supplement income from sources other than legal employment. However, how do individuals form expectations about their earnings potential in the labor market? If there is a considerable gap between what
the individual believes is attainable (group experience) and what is unattainable
(larger society experience), an individual perceives this gap as relative deprivation. Hence the opportunity costs of crime may be reduced because the returns from regular employment are seen as minimal. In contrast, if the larger society also suffers from unemployment, the shortage of employment opportunities may still be considered equitable. attention that crimes, such as burglary or theft, receive in comparison with white collar crime, although the latter type of crimes represent a larger
proportion of monetary losses than the former type.

Crime accompanies social life from its very beginning – it occurs in every society and in every stage of its development, regardless of its structure, system or historical period. Undoubtedly, crime is a consequence of many social and economic problems which
constantly change, therefore there are so many controversial and unresolved issued connected with the influence of social and economical factors on crime. This article is an attempt to find an answer to whether the socio-economic factors clearly have a substantial impact on

crime.

Regardless of whether we like it or not – crime is a constant component of our life. The crime level is influenced by lots of factors

which nature is heterogeneous. Among them, we may distinguish the socio - economic situation of the offender. Statistics (not only Polish) seem to confirm the assumption that there is a strong connection between social and economic conditions and the level of crime .

● SOCIO - ECONOMIC FACTORS CAUSES CRIME RATE INCREASES

Crime and changes in the structure of crime are both affected by such elements as: the degree of economic development, socio - political system that functions in a given country, the progress of industrialization and urbanization, transformations in social structure which are age-related to members of the society and finally, migrations. Transformations may be carried out in a revolutionary way or throughout

a longer period of time, they can also occur suddenly as a result of some turbulent changeovers and rapid changes which happen in a given community.

In the case of our country one should consider political changes, accompanied by destabilizing and disintegrative processes, political changes with the transition from a communist to a democratic regime. Further modifications were related to the economic system, changes in ownership structure and the emergence of structural unemployment .New conditions caused a shift in social structure, namely, new social groups were

formed, social hierarchy was changed, and many social groups suffered economic degradation.

● The influence of socio - economic factors on crime

Therefore, one should ask a question whether in fact the economic situation shapes the level of crime rate . While being under constant modifications and transformations, society will never stay unchanged. Changes in the number, gender, age structure, migration (demographic changes) also have their mutual influence related to the economy, system of power, education, health protection, religion, and crime. Poor economic situation may translate into crime by an increase in unemployment. It should be noted
that unemployment, naturally connected with the economy may have a different dimension. We distinguish between the structural, cyclical, long-term, and frictional unemployment. Because of the social and demographic factors, such as gender, age or education level of people affected by the unemployment, there may be various relationships and impact on criminal activity.An analysis of police statistics shows that the highest intensity of crime occurs among unemployed people who are under thirty years of age . If an individual is affected by long-term unemployment, he or she starts to be affected by the consequences of such a situation, namely a sense of exclusion, injustice, and finally the lack of hope of finding a legitimate source of income . The analysis shows that unemployment brings on crime
against property rather than violence . However, it should be noted that the increase in unemployment in various ways may affect particular social groups by increasing or decreasing their criminal activity. At this point one should outline four specific relationships between unemployment and crime as below:

· Some offenders combine their legal professional work with criminal activity. Legal business is treated as a camouflage for illegal operation. In this case, the development of unemployment may reduce the "gray zone" business, as the legal work, in this case, gives a sense of security for conducting criminal activity.

· There is a number of crimes, possible to be committed only during conducting activities while being legally employed, for example: "handing over bribes to officials", "employee theft". In those situations the growth of unemployment will inhibit the number of crimes of the above mentioned type, rather than increase them.

· Young people, in particular distinguish between two options: being legally employed, or being involved in a criminal activity. If the lack of work prevails, the willingness to take an income from illegal sources may be decisive. Unemployment, in this perspective may cause an increase in crime.

· There are people for whom unemployment is strictly related to their living style. This group of people treat legal work as an abnormal situation – those people are not part of the labor market. For them, the lack of employment is part of their cultural identity, and criminal activity is, in their environment, a socially accepted source of income. In this case, an increase in unemployment will have no influence on the formation of criminal behavior.

Further analysis of inter-relations of factors related to the discussed problem may incline to believe that in a period of an economic recession, a higher level of crime against property and lower against the person is being observed, whereas, during a period of prosperity (an economic boom) the situation is

other way round: higher level of crime against the person and lower against property is being distinguished. Apart from unemployment other economic factors such as:

poverty, the level, dynamics and diversity of earnings and the pace of economic development influence the crime rate. Poverty has long been the factor which has been strongly associated with criminal activity. As it was indicated by Alain Peyrefitte, "crime is the child of poverty".

While trying to explain the influence of socio - economic changes on crime, a number of changes in the economic system should be taken into account, such as the emergence of
economic crises, periods of economic prosperity, the processes of European unification, EU enlargement, globalization, the processes of industrialization and urbanization. If the economic components affect almost all types of social activity, there must be a link between them and the crime. Conditions, economic tension may create some situations, often stressful situations that may facilitate criminal activity . Initially, the analysis of the relationship between social and economic transformation and changes in the crime indicated that there is a causal connection, but now this assumption is not so obvious. One may only unquestionably
talk about correlation between a group of various factors, also non-economical and certain types of crime. A good economic situation, a period of prosperity may both influence either increase or decrease in the number of offenses.

First of all, it may increase the possibility to commit a crime as the easiness and availability of products make them an easy target for a thief or even a person who has a desire to steal an item without really the need to have it. Abundance of goods cause that products may become an object of a crime (e.g become vandalized). Furthermore, if people have too much leisure, they tend to change their

lifestyle – and this change is associated with taking part in or participate in events or actions with other people. This causes a greater opportunity for people to be involved in a prohibited
actions and crimes against the person. A period of prosperity may, on the other hand decrease the possibility to commit a crime as people stick to generally accepted social standards and the desire to commit an illegal actions e.g. theft, swindle is reduced. They feel more socially secured and safe. The better social and economic status people have, the lower need to be involved in something prohibited by law. In case of a well-paid job, also motivational elements appear as well as the fear of the
consequences of a wrongful act. In literature of this field, there is no evidence that there is a connection between the level of crime and the level of industrialization. However, there is a strong connection between the level of crime and spatial mobility of the population, and the size of migration.

The internationalization of crime causes intensification of organized crime. Possibilities to commit a crime also change – smuggling, tax frauds, economic crime, production of drugs and weapon, money frauds, prostitution, ?money laundering", customs offenses, corruption. The changing structure of crime, its forms and ways of committing it indicate a real change in social structure and transformations of the social life as well as missing norms and values of
societies which in a given historical period may be observed.

In conclusion,the discussed and analyzed socio - economic factors incline to believe that social and economical sphere of human life is interrelated and interdependent. There are certain correlations with the crime level and social behavior as well as with economy and human vulnerability to commit an offense. However, careful The influence of socio - economic factors on crime examination in this respect is still needed. Causal dependencies which occur in societies on every stage of their development are difficult to explain.So how to carry out on the research, analysis of recovery plans and criminal statistics as well as literature allowed to form a conclusion that people should not only focus on individuals in crime prevention programs but on such forms of activity that would be targeted to whole societies. Preventive measures should aim at reducing both economic and social inequalities, e.g balance the level of income or promote social cohesion. Although various crime preventive strategies and programs continue to be developed , they may only reduce crime rate on a small scale, basically they will not have a clear influence on the increase or decrease in a criminal activity in a particular country or in a global dimension as too many social and economic factors should be taken into account.

IV

Is poor macro economic environment a main root to crime causation

Is poor macro economic environment cause crime essentially? Economic Theories indicate the roots of crime are diverse and a discipline like economics, predicated on rational behavior, may be at something of a disadvantage in explaining a phenomenon largely viewed as irrational. A recent survey suggests that three general issues are of central concern in the economics of crime literature: the effects of incentives on criminal behavior, how decisions interact in a market-setting, and the use of cost-benefit analysis to assess alternative policies to reduce crime will focus on the role of incentives on criminal behavior.

However, trend in criminal participation rates in most industrialized economies is a difficult task. Many social scientists argue that crime is closely related to work, education and poverty and that truancy, youth unemployment
and crime are by products or even measures of social exclusion. "Blue-collar"criminals often have limited education and possess limited labor market skills. These characteristics partly explain the poor employment records and low legitimate earnings of most criminals. These sort of issues originally led economists to examine the relationship between wages and unemployment rates on crime. More recently
economists have also considered the benefits and costs of educational programs to
reduce crime.

A related question concerns the impact of sanctions. For example, does increased imprisonment lower the crime rate? How does the deterrent effect of formal sanctions arise? Although criminologists have been tackling such issues for many years, it is only recently that economists have entered the arena of controversy. This is not surprising given the high levels of crime and the associated allocation of public and private resources towards crime prevention. The expenditure on the criminal justice system (police, prisons, prosecution/defense and courts) is a significant proportion of government budgets. In addition, firms and households are spending
increasingly more on private security.
The incentive-based economic model of crime is a model of decision making in risky situations.

Economists analyse the way in which individual attitudes toward risk affect the extent of illegal behavior. In most of the early literature, the economic models of crime are single-period individual choice models. These models generally see the individual as deciding to allocate time with criminal activity as one possible use of time. A key feature is the notion of utility; judgements are made of the likely gain to be realised (the 'expected utility') from a particular choice of action. Individuals are assumed to be rational decision-makers who engage in either legal or illegal activities according to the expected utility from each activity. An individual's participation in illegal activity is, therefore, explained by the opportunity cost of illegal activity (for example, earnings from legitimate work), factors that influence the returns to illegal activity (for example, detection and the severity of punishment), and by tastes and preferences for illegal activity.

Economists see criminal activity as being similar to paid employment in that it requires time and produces an income. Clearly, the dichotomy between either criminal activity or legal activity is an oversimplification. For example, individuals could engage in criminal activities while employed since they have greater opportunities to commit crime; similarly, some criminals may jointly supplement work income with crime income in order to satisfy their needs. A secondary problem with the economist's choice model, which was highlighted in our opening comments, is that young people are more likely to participate in crime long before they participate in the labor market. This observation raises questions about the appropriateness of the economic model of crime in explaining juvenile crime.

Economic models of criminal behavior have focused on sanction effects (e.g. deterrence issue) and the relationship between work and crime. In the main, these models have not directly addressed the role of education in offending. It could be argued that unemployment is the conduit through which other factors influence the crime rate. For example, poor educational attainment may be highly correlated with the incidence of crime. However, this may also be a key determinant of unemployment. Although educational variables have been included as covariates with crime rates, they have not received a great deal of attention in correlational studies.

To the basic theory ,economic Model of Criminal Behavior: Basic theory is

as mentioned in the overview, the economic model of crime is a standard model of decision making where individuals choose between criminal activity and legal activity on the basis of the expected utility from those acts. It is assumed that participation in criminal activity is the result of an optimizing individual responding to incentives. Among the factors that influence an individual's decision to engage in criminal activities are (i) the expected gains from crime relative to earnings from legal work (ii) the chance (risk) of being caught and convicted, (iii) the extent of punishment and (iv) the opportunities in legal activities. Specifying an equation to capture the incentives in the criminal decision is a natural first step in most analyses

of the crime as work models. The most important of these gives the relative rewards

of legal and illegal activity. For example, the economic

model sees the criminal as committing a crime if the expected gain from criminal activity exceeds the gain from legal activity, generally work.

Just as in benefit-cost analysis, when comparing alternative strategies, interest centers on the returns from one decision vis-a-vis returns from another decision. For example, a preference for crime over work implies the earnings gap between legal and illegal activities must rise when the probability of being caught and the severity of punishment increases. Attitudes towards risk are central to economic models of criminal choice. For example, if the individual is said to dislike risk (i.e., to be risk averse) then he will respond more to changes in the chances of being apprehended than to changes in the extent of punishment, other things being equal. Becker developed a comparative-static model that considered primarily the deterrent effect of the criminal justice system. As we will see, how individuals respond to deterrent and incapacitation effects of sanctions has generated considerable theoretical and empirical interest from economists.

Thus, severe sentencing and improvements in legal work opportunities of criminals must be expected jointly to reduce crime. Of course, this assumes that crime and work are determined by the same factors and that higher legitimate earnings increase the probability of working. In the early literature, economists applied static one period time allocation models to analyse criminal behavior. In other words, crime and work are assumed to be substitute activities; if an individual allocates more time to work, he will commit less crime because he will have less time to do so. The basic economic model of crime is static or comparative static in economic jargon because it does not see the potential criminal as considering more than a single time period when making his decision.

Early studies of criminal behavior by economists can be criticized for being set in a static framework. Economic models of crime are typically estimated as static models, though there are many reasons to suspect dynamic effects matter, both theoretically through habit formation, interdependence of preferences, capital accumulation, addiction, peer group effects, etc., and empirically through improvements in fit when lagged dependent variables or autocorrelated residuals are included in the model. Labor economists have long been interested in state dependence, the fact that activities chosen in the current period may be strongly affected by the individual's activities in the previous period.

Flinn incorporates human capital formation in a time-allocation model. In his model, human capital is accumulated at work, not at school. Consequently, crime takes time away from work and hence diminishes the amount of human capital accumulated. The diminished human capital leads to lower future wages and hence less time spent working. Since crime and work are substitutes in his model, the decline in time allocated to work leads to increased participation in criminal activities.

In nowadays global labor market, the basic idea underlying the model is that young men have two types of jobs available to them –skilled and unskilled – where wage profiles are rising in the former (due to accumulation of human capital, training and experience) and flat in the latter (no training). If discounted wages are equalized across jobs, the unskilled wage would start above and end below skilled wage. Also, human capital theory suggests that job stability will be greater in skilled sector than in the unskilled sector. Given these predictions, and assuming that a criminal conviction adversely affects prospects of getting a skilled job, it is likely that conviction is associated with higher pay and higher job instability. So, low skillful workers usually do criminal behaviors more than high skillful workers in our societies nowadays.

Concerning how to examine the impact of legitimate labor market experiences (e.g., unemployment) and sanctions on criminal behavior whether they have relationship question? Broadly speaking, the empirical findings are that (i) poor legitimate labor market opportunities of potential criminals, such as low wages and high rates of unemployment, increases the supply of criminal activities and (ii) sanctions deter crime.

Unemployment could be taken to influence the opportunity cost of illegal activity. High rates of unemployment growth could be taken to imply a restriction on the availability of legal activities, and thus serve to ultimately reduce the opportunity cost of engaging in illegal activities. Although theoretically well-defined,
most empirical studies of the unemployment-crime relationship have provided mixed
evidence. Instead of primarily
focusing on crime as a function of unemployment, they use a richer set of controls, like deterrence, employment status, age, education, race and neighbourhood
characteristics.

One problem with most work and crime models is that they assume both
activities are mutually exclusive. This may be a problematic assumption when considering disadvantaged youths. The fact that a youth can shift from crime to an unskilled job and back again or can commit crime while holding a legal job means that the supply of youths to crime will be quite elastic with respect to relative rewards from crime vis-a-vis legal work or to the number of criminal opportunities. From the 1970s through the 1990s the labor market prospects for unskilled workers in most OECD countries has deteriorated considerably. In particular, the real
earnings of young unskilled men fell, while income inequality rose. This suggests that
as the earnings gap widens, relative deprivation increases, which in turn leads to
increases in crime.

A substantial problem that has been ignored in the vast majority of empirical
studies is nonstationarity of crime rates. A time-series is

said to be nonstationary if (1) the mean and/or variance does not remain constant over time and (2) covariance between observations depends on the time at which they occur. In the US, the index crime rate appears strongly nonstationary, for the most part being integrated of order one with both deterministic and stochastic trends (a random variable whose mean value and variance are time-dependent is said to follow a stochastic trend) .The empirical results suggest a long-run equilibrium relationship between crime, prison population, female labor supply and durable consumption.

The explanatory variables include the number of juveniles or adults in custody per crime; the number of juveniles or adults in custody per juvenile or adult; economic variables, including the state unemployment rate and demographic variables, including race and legal drinking age, and dummy variables for year and state. Levitt finds that juvenile crime is negatively related to the severity of penalties, and that juvenile offenders are at least as responsive to sanctions as adults. Interestingly, he finds that the difference between the punishments given to youths and adults helps explain sharp changes in crimes committed by youths as they reach the age of majority.

Most economic work on crime has focused on the deterrent effect of the criminal justice system and on the interrelationship between work and crime. Empirical work provides some, but not unambiguous support for the deterrence hypothesis. Recent work by economist suggest that the relationship between work and crime may be far more complicated than implied by economic models.

The rise in juvenile crime rates has focused increasing attention on youth crime. This has forced economists to expand their thinking to incorporate such things as education, peer group effects and the influence of family and community. Increasingly both theoretical and empirical work on the economics of crime has come to use dynamic models. Theoretical work is developing multi-period models of crime. Empirically economists are using both panel data techniques and modern time series techniques to examine the dynamics of criminal behavior.

- CRIMINOLOGICAL THEORIES ABOUT

why people commit crime are used—and misused, if poor global economic environment factor was main factor causes people do criminal behaviors?

Every day by legislative policy makers
and community corrections managers when
they develop new initiatives, sanctions, and
programs; and these theories are also being
applied—and misapplied—by line community
corrections officers in the workplace as
they classify, supervise, counsel, and control
offenders placed on their caseloads. The
purpose of this article is to provide a brief
overview of the major theories of crime causation and then to consider the implications of these criminological theories for current and
future community corrections practice. Four
distinct groups of theories will be examined:
classical theories, biological theories, psychological theories, and sociological theories of crime causation. While the
assumptions of classical criminology have
been used to justify a wide range of sentencing

and corrections policies and practices over the past several decades, it is also possible to identify the influence of other theories of crime causation on corrections policies and practices during this same period.

As we examine each group of theories, we consider how—and why—the basic functions of probation and parole officers change based on the theory of crime causation under review.

When considering the link between theory and practice, it is important to remember the following basic truth: Criminologists disagree about both the causes and solutions to our crime problem. This does not mean that criminologists have little to offer to probation and parole officers in terms of practical advice; to other community corrections programs are to the contrary, we think a discussion of "cause" is be successful as "people changing" agencies. Critical to the ongoing debate over the appro- But can we reasonably expect such diversity priate use of community-based sanctions, and flexibility from community corrections and the development of effective community agencies, or is it more likely that one theory— corrections policies, practices, and programs. or group of theories—will be the dominant.

However, the degree of uncertainty on the influence on community corrections practice? cause—or causes—of our crime problem in Based on recent reviews of United States academic community suggests that a rections history, we suspect that one group of certain degree of skepticism is certainly in theories—supported by a dominant political order when "new" crime control strategies are ideology—will continue to dominate until introduced. We need to look carefully at the the challenges to its efficacy move the field— theory of crime causation on which these new both ideologically and theoretically—in a new initiatives are based. It is our view that since direction. We may—or may not—be at such a each group of theories we describe is appli- watershed point in the United States today.

An Overview of Criminological Theories

Classically-based criminologists explain criminal behavior as a conscious choice by individuals based on an assessment of the costs and benefits of various forms of criminal activity. Biologically-based criminologists explain criminal behavior as determined—in part—by the presence of certain inherited traits that may increase the likelihood of criminal behavior.

Psychologically-based criminologists explain criminal behavior as the consequence of individual factors, such as negative early childhood experiences and inadequate socialization, that result in criminal thinking patterns and/or incomplete cognitive development.

Sociologically-based criminologists explain criminal behavior as primarily influenced by a variety of community-level factors that appear to be related—both directly and indirectly—to the high level of crime in some of our (often poorest) communities, including blocked legitimate opportunity, the existence of subcultural values that support criminal behavior, a breakdown of community-level informal social controls, and an unjust system of criminal laws and criminal justice.

To a classical criminologist, the answer is simple: The benefits of law breaking (such as money, property, revenge, and status) simply outweigh the potential costs/consequences of getting caught and convicted. When viewed from a classical perspective, we are all capable of committing crime in a given situation, but we make a rational decision (to act or desist) based on our analysis of the costs and benefits of the action. If this is true, then it is certainly possible to deter a potential offender by (1) developing a system of "sentencing" in which the punishment outweighs the (benefit of the) crime, and (2) ensuring both punishment certainty and celerity through efficient police and court administration. "Classical" theories of criminal behavior are appealing to criminal justice policy makers, because they are based on the premise that the key to solving the crime problem is to have a strong system of formal social control. In other words, the classical theorist believes that the system can make a difference, regardless of the myriad of individual and social ills that exist. During the past four decades, a number of federal, state, and local programs have been initiated to improve the deterrent capacity of the criminal justice system, including proactive police strategies to ensure greater certainty of apprehension,priority prosecution/speedy trial strategies to ensure greater celerity (speed) in the court process, and determinate/mandatory sentencing strategies to ensure greater punishment certainty and severity.

To further our deterrent aims, we have significantly increased our institutional capacity during this same period and passed legislation that includes mandatory minimum periods of incarceration for drug-related crimes, while simultaneously developing a series of surveillance-oriented intermediate sanctions (e.g., intensive probation supervision, electronic monitoring/house arrest) for a subgroup of the offenders under community supervision.

It is apparent from these initiatives that classical assumptions about crime causation are still being used as the basis for current crime control strategies. Some have argued that our four-decade-long emphasis on "deterrencebased"crime control policies has resulted in safer communities; in fact, by most standard measures (crime rates, victimization rates) we have less crime and less violence today than at any point since the early 1970s.

With most experts estimating that about a quarter of the crime decline can be linked to tougher sentencing policies, while three quarters of the decline have been attributed to other factors (such as the economy, education, and immigration). A careful review of the evaluation research indicates that community-based sanctions does not support the notion that increased surveillance and control reduces recidivism (that is, an offender's likelihood of rearrest, reconviction, and/ or re-incarceration). There are two possible explanations for these findings: (1) the underlying assumptions of classical criminologists (i.e., most people are rational, and weigh the costs and benefits of various acts in the same manner) are wrong (e.g., people commit crimes for emotional reasons, because of mental illness, and/or because they believe the criminal act is justified, given circumstances and prevailing community values); or (2) the current sentencing strategies and community corrections programs need to be even tougher
and deterrence-oriented (in other words, the
theory is correct; it just has not been implemented

correctly).

While community corrections populations and probation rates also remain high, and continue to use multiple conditions that emphasize surveillance and control
(through drug testing, electronic monitoring, curfews, and now social media monitoring).
For example, in the name of deterrence, legislation has been passed in several states
allowing the lifetime supervision of paroled.
The final group of psychological theories focuses on the potential link between personality and criminality. Although there is currently much debate on whether personality characteristics play a significant role in
determining subsequent criminal behavior, a number of prominent criminologists have
argued that "the root causes of crime are not...social issues [high unemployment, bad
schools] but deeply ingrained features of the human personality and its early experiences.
Low intelligence, an impulsive personality, and a lack of empathy for other people are
among the leading individual characteristics of people at risk for becoming offenders".

- THE IMPACT OF CRIMINOLOGICAL THEORY WHETHER POOR ECONOMIC ENVIRONMENT IS THE REAL REASON TO INFLUENCE CRIME RATE RAISES

This question concerns to how to implement and the development of strategies
to assess community "risk" and then relocate
offenders who currently reside in "high-risk"

neighborhoods to lower-risk areas, utilizing the lure of new job opportunities or housing incentives. A final group of sociological theories of crime causation can be identified, based on the premise that people become criminals not because of some inherent characteristic, personality defect, or other sociologically-based "pressure" or influence, but because of decisions made by those in positions of power in government, especially those in the criminal justice system. The social strategies implementation to reduce crime rate increases may include as below:

Intervention Strategy

(1) Strategies emphasize education, skill development, and employment opportunity.

(2) Strategies emphasize community-level value change, alternatives to gang involvement, and offender relocation.

(3) Strategies target improving community structural conditions, resource availability, and collective efficacy; strengthening informal community social control mechanisms; and eliminating poverty pockets.

(4) Strategies focus on the breakdown of informal social control mechanisms—attachment, commitment, involvement, and belief—and

emphasize the importance of the relationship between the offender and his/her probation/parole officer.

(5) Strategies designed to target the turning points in the lifecourse that have been directly related to desistance among adult offenders—marriage, employment, military service, and offender relocation.

(6) Strategies focus on the use of alternative dispute/ conflict resolution strategies that result in lower levels of formal criminal justice system involvement in the lives of community residents; and on the application of community/ restorative justice principles in traditional criminal justice settings, including community corrections.

All these strategies are supposed that the country's crime rate raises is not due to poor economic environment factor influence mainly. The country's crime rate raising is based on other non economic related factors influence.

Given the potential negative consequences of labeling,we need to ask ourselves: (1) which laws do we really need to enforce? and (2) which offenders can (and should) we divert from the formal court process?

A number of observers have suggested probation and parole officers do not have an adequate "professional base" to do the job we ask them to do. However, it is our view that it is impossible to assess the qualifications of community corrections personnel unless we first clearly define the primary job orientation of the community corrections officer: Do we want our line staff to emphasize treatment or control? As we have indicated throughout this article, how we answer the "why" (or causation) question (Why did the offender commit this crime?) will determine not only our general orientation toward certain categories of crime (e.g., drug offenses, violent crime) and groups of offenders (e.g., sex offenders, gang members, drunk drivers), but also the types of functions we will expect community corrections to perform.

A number of line probation and parole officers only have an undergraduate
degree, while some have even less formal education. This diversity in educational background would be a cause for concern if we could clearly establish a relationship between education and the job itself. Unfortunately, we do not have a firm grasp on the types of skills necessary to be an effective probation or parole officer in the next decade. While a number of "get tough" intermediate sanctions programs have been developed based on classical assumptions about crime control (e.g., intensive supervision, house arrest, boot camps), these programs still include only a small percentage (approximately 10 percent) of all offenders under community supervision. If these programs continue to expand, it appears that we will need to draw our POs from the pool of undergraduate criminal justice majors,

perhaps requiring some prior experience as a police officer or corrections guard. Such "deskilling" is an inevitable consequence of the movement away from treatment and toward the technology of control.

In conclusion, if some countries feel their crime rate raising reason is not caused by poor economic environment factor, they can attempt to apply above strategies to solve crime rating problems to investigate whether poor economic environment factor is the main factor to influence their crime rate raising in possible.

The relationship between poor economics environment and high crime rate

I believe that whether the country has better or worse welfare economic environment or its welfare is improved to satisfy its citizen's living of standard, it will bring effect whether its society's crime rate is more less. I shall explain why and how the country welfare will influence its crime rate to be increased or decreased as below reasons:

What does the new welfare economics mean? It can be explained that how the county citizens interpersonal comparison of utility and social welfare function to their country's welfare policy to let they feel more satisfactory or less satisfactory. Their satisfaction can include leisure and non-leisure consumption satisfaction daily. So, if the country can give more welfares to let its citizen to feel more satisfaction on leisure and consumption aspects. Then, they won't choose to do any crime activities more easily.

In fact, economists have used no methods of scientific research in arriving at their conclusions about whether the country can provide better or worse economic welfare, which can influence the society's crime rate is raised or decreased. However, I shall attempt to explain that why any country's welfare can let its citizen to satisfy more or less, then it can influence the country's crime rate to be increased or decreased.

Every country's economic welfare was said to be a part of total welfare, as well as it can be brought directly or indirectly into relation with money. Why do some countries change their social welfare, then their crime rate can be improved to reduce really? In other words, a less satisfaction to a man with more money than it will to one with less money. Based on this assumption, when the country has good welfare to provide the low income people, then they will feel more satisfaction on their daily living needs. They won't feel worry their basic foods, living needs. Consequently, the society will increase many low income people , they won't feel difficulty to live, then stealing , fighting etc. opposed social crime behaviors or activities will ought to be decreased, due to the low income people feel or believe their country can feel what they have real essential needs at the moment. The low income people can feel safe to live in the country. Then, the country's crime rate ought to be decreased. So, it seems that crime rate increases or decreases, it has relationship between the country's welfare satisfaction to their essential needs, in specially the low income group.

Why does poor welfare influence the low Income people do crime behaviors more easily? It is simple, for example, when two consumers , they enter the supermarket to make choice to buy apples to eat. When the high income consumer performs to take any good taste apples to buy to eat. The another low income consumer or unemployed consumer , he looks the another consumer is taking any good taste apples to choose which one is the best apple to buy. During their apply choice process, the low income Or unemployed apple consumer will feel unhappy when he knows the another consumer had chosen the most good taste apples to buy to eat in the supermarket. However, due to the country can not provide the better welfare to support the low income or poor person or unemployed person has enough money to buy any good taste apples to eat in the supermarket. Then, the lacking enough social welfare person , he will do stealing apples crime behavior in the supermarket more easily if he brings one plastic bags. So, if the country has many low income people or poor people or unemployed people are living in the country, they feel that their government can not provide enough welfare to support their essential living need. Then, they will choose to do crime behaviors more easily. Consequently, the country's crime rate will also be raised in possible.

So, I believe that any country's crime rate is more or less, it has relationship to its low income people whether they feel their country government can give more or less welfare to support their basic daily living needs in order to do any crime behavior more easily. Because one individual's happiness is also , to some extent, dependent on what others consume. Obviously, the standard of living or welfare level of his family is not a matter of indifference to a man. But we do not avoid the difficulty by taking family as a unit. So, when the country has many families are living, if there are many families' fathers , they are not employing or they are often working in the low income level as well as they government can not provide enough welfares to support their living need. It will bring that they feel living pressure to support their children to learn and wife's living need, if their wives are housewives role or without job housewives. So, low income or poor families will do crime behaviors more easily to compare single people, because single people do not need to support their wives and children living cost. So, if the country's families householder group number is more than single householder group number, then the country ought concentrate on supporting more welfare to the householder families group living needs to reduce their living pressure, e.g. children education assistance, handicapped assistance, low income short time welfare assistance, wife short time unemployed assistance or wife low income assistance. When , they feel lesser living pressure from their government's welfare assistance. Then, these low income families won't do any family fighting or violence or killing themselves families crime behaviors more easily in society.

So, when the country can improved its welfare to be better, then it can encourage many low income people have ability to consume. It will bring its business and economic environment to be better. So, it has case and effect relationship between welfare and economic environment and crime rate to any countries. The most realistic general assumption , we can make is that, when a man saves he is normally saving up to buy a collection similar in composition to that which he is buying when he saves. Therefore, when comparing his welfare for, says, two different years, we must , in effect, scale up his expenditure in the one year until it is equal to his income of that year, and then ask whether, in the other year, he could have bought the scaled-up collection of the one year.

So, every country's government needs to arrange the reasonable welfare to give the different living needs people in itself country. It can ask this question in order to evaluate every low income or poor people's real welfare need, the question is : Could the poor or low income person have bought last year's collection of goods? So, the country government can gather every poor or low income welfare need applicants' past year consumption or purchase price, kinds of product information, e.g. the low income or poor welfare assistance applicant whether he had enough income to buy any electric products , e.g. desktop, laptop computer(s), television, wash machine, fan, air condition etc. home electric products for his family to use last year. If the welfare assistance applicant had any last year electric products purchase record, then I believe that he still have enough income to support his family living, because these are not his basic living need. It means that he ought have enough money to support his family living need in this year. In simple, his welfare assistance ought be less amount to other welfare assistance applicants, they had not bought any home electric products for their families to use last year. So, it is one good evaluation method to assess whether government ought give how much welfare assistance to every welfare assistance applicant in our societies nowadays. Instead, how many number of children number to the families, old age parents are living with or without living to their sons or daughters together, how many children , they are studying primary, secondary or university etc. families member living dependence factor will also need to be considered to assess every family welfare assistance needs. However, it is reasonable that when the family has many lacking independent ability of members who are living together, then this family ought be provided more welfare assistance need to compare the family has many independent ability of members who are living together, because when family has many independent members are living together, they must have more income source to compare the family has less independent members are living members are living together. It means that the family total income must be enough to support whose living need more easily to compare the less number independent family member case.

Thus, welfare economics and ethics can not then , be separated. They are inseparable because the welfare is a value terminology. The answer is that it could be such a system was held to be anything, for example, welfare or happiness, it would once again be emotive and ethical. The subject is one about which nothing interesting can be said without value judgements, for the reason that every country government needs take a moral interest in welfare and happiness to let it poor people or low income people feel less living pressure, when they can feel their government is really considerate their living needs. Also if we propose to use a certain criterion for an increase the economic welfare of an individual, then the country ought can raise the poor or low income people's consumption ability or consumption desires. Consequently, when their consumption behaviors are encouraged to raise any kinds of products are sold easily from them. The country's economy will be improved to be better. Then, the stealing crime cases will also cause to be decreased directly.

In conclusion, I believe that these above cases can explain that why it have direct relationship between welfare economy and consumer behavior and crime rate. Every country government ought considerate how to arrange the reasonable welfare level to satisfy the different real welfare need applicants' real living needs in order to avoid unfair welfare assistance treatment to let every welfare assistance applicant feel unfair and angry to themselves country government. Thus, welfare economy has real relationship to influence every country's consumer behaviors or consumption desires to be increase or decrease as well as their crime behavioral causation.

Printed by Libri Plureos GmbH in Hamburg,
Germany